UNDERSTANDING PUPPY TESTING

It's been almost 20 years since I first performed a puppy aptitude test. In these two decades, I have been fortunate enough to test a wide variety of breeds: Goldens, Labs, Westies, Norfolk and Norwich Terriers, Pointers, Brittanys, Great Pyrenees, Dalmatians, Corgis, Boxers, Schnauzers, Samoyeds, French Bulldogs, German Shepherds, Springer Spaniels, Dobermans, Collies, Shelties, Leonbergers, Dachshunds, Portugese Water Dogs, and several mixed breed litters. I have been asked to test litters for breeders, and have often tested litters for buyers. As a breeder of German Shepherds, I have my own litters tested to gather additional insight into each puppy before placement.

In 1977, I was introduced to puppy testing when I began work for Guiding Eyes for the Blind in Yorktown Heights, New York as part of the staff at the breeding farm where Labradors, Goldens and German Shepherds were bred for their futures as guide dogs. At any given time, there were

Understanding Puppy Testing

six to eight litters at the farm, all at various ages ranging from newborns to 8 week old puppies.

At 8 weeks of age, puppies were delivered to their foster homes who would raise them for 11-15 months (depending upon the breed and the particular bloodlines). But before being placed, each puppy was individually given a Puppy Test which offered some predictive clues about that puppy's potential as a guide dog. Part of my job, in addition to breeding and whelping activities, was to perform puppy tests.

Suzanne Clothier

 History of Puppy Testing

Puppy testing was developed by Guide Dogs for the Blind, Inc., in San Rafael, California as a way of evaluating whether certain characteristics desirable in a guide dog had been inherited. This was not a simple undertaking, and initially, the tests devised did not work.

Clarence Pfaffenberger, who was involved with the initial efforts, says in his book, **The New Knowledge of Dog Behavior**:

> *"To our dismay, we found that after we had developed tests based upon giving our puppies a simulated experience of what they would have to do as Guide Dogs, some of our highest test puppies were among those who failed in training. What was even more disconcerting was that in training these same puppies, now adults, showed all the good qualities their tests had predicted. Their failure was due to the fact . . . that they would not take responsibility of making a decision for their master . . . It was many years before we learned that this matter of self confidence is instilled in the puppy by what happens to it very early in life."*

Understanding Puppy Testing

Fortunately, Pfaffenberger and his associates did not give up, but went on. Turning to guide dog trainers, they asked for and received a list of reasons of why dogs failed:

> 1. Mentally dull, does not take an interest in his lessons
> 2. Ear sensitivity dull, slow to react to sounds
> 3. Body sensitivity dull, does not seem to feel corrections
> 4. Smarty, thinks it knows everything already
> 5. Ear sensitivity too acute, shies at noises
> 6. Too body sensitive, constantly afraid of corrections
> 7. Has a fawning personality, always pays more attention to his trainer, personally, than to what he is being taught
> 8. Afraid of persons or moving objects, especially wheeled objects
> 9. Not aware of persons or moving wheeled objects, will run into them or allow them to run into him
> 10. Bites, especially because he is afraid
> 11. Too stubborn to be taught
> 12. Lacks stability, will act one way one day and, under similar circumstances, will act entirely different another.

Using this list as a guideline, Pfaffenberger and associates went on to develop tests that would shed light on those various character traits. By 1954, when making a thorough analysis of their tests, Dr. John Fuller who, along with Dr. J.P. Scott, had been doing ground breaking research on developmental periods in the dog at Bar Harbor, Maine, asked if Pfaffenberger had noticed a correlation between scores on the fetch test and ultimate success as Guide Dogs. They discovered that puppies with good scores on both the fetch test and the two-wheeled cart test (where pups were approached by a little cart) were also the puppies who almost never failed in training. (The exceptions were puppies who did well on those tests but had poor temperament otherwise.)

Through refinement of the testing process and extraordinary record keeping, Guide Dogs for the Blind was able to dramatically improve the success rate for their breeding program by selectively breeding the dogs who demonstrated and passed on the qualities desirable in the guide dog.

Understanding Puppy Testing

 Puppy Testing Today

At this time, several versions of the original puppy test exist. Using Pfaffenberger's work as a guide, other trainers, such as Bill Campbell, Michael Fox and Wendy Volhard, developed tests which recognized that there is a wide range of individual characteristics, and that while one puppy might be unsuitable as a guide dog, he might serve very well as a companion animal. Qualities such as high energy or noise sensitivity, which might make a dog less than ideal for one family, might be just the ticket for another.

Puppy testing can be a useful guide for matching puppies and buyers. In my last litter, for example, there were seven puppies. All of them had excellent temperament, but each puppy had a unique blend of characteristics. For the family with pre-teen children buying their first dog, they needed a puppy who was not noise sensitive (kids can be noisy), relatively touch insensitive (kids can be clumsy), willing to take direction (kids need to be able to control a large working breed) and very people oriented with medium energy.

Puppy testing did not make my decision for me, but it did confirm what I had observed all along - that the sweet, mild female was the correct choice for this family. What puppy would they have chosen for themselves? The most dominant, high energy female who believed, and still does, that she owns the world. Fortunately for both the family and the puppies, the high powered pup went to an experienced handler who wanted and got a "Maserati" of a dog.

 Breeders & Buyers

Today, breeders and buyers both use puppy testing for a variety of reasons. For some breeders, puppy testing offers an outside, fairly objective opinion of their puppies' behavior, and confirmation or refinement of their own knowledge of the puppies. Others, though well intentioned, believe that puppy testing will neatly define which puppy should go where. Often unaware of the limits of such testing, these are the breeders who present me with a list of prospective homes and ask me which puppy should go to which home. They are never pleased when I tell them that they do not have a puppy suitable for a particular home.

But my favorite remains the breeder who happily informs you that they do their own testing! While aware that puppy testing is somehow desirable, these breeders are ignorant of the basics which dictate that the tester must be someone unknown to the litter. Testing your own litter is a lot like auditing your own books.

Understanding Puppy Testing

Buyers believe testing will help them find their perfect puppy. To a certain extent, they are correct that puppy testing can help them either include or reject a puppy as a candidate. Misled by any number of books that urge the reader to perform these "simple" tests, buyers are sometimes surprised when breeders refuse to let a well meaning but inexperienced buyer test their litter. While there are some breeders who refuse to have their puppies tested, most are either unknowledgeable about testing or unwilling, and wisely so, to have an inexperienced person working with highly impressionable puppies. (These same breeders may be quite agreeable to working with a reputable and experienced tester.)

Should the breeder agree, the buyer who does the test without experience or considerable input from an experience tester is much like the average car owner going out to look over a used car. The little signs that a knowledgeable mechanic would recognize and know to look for may very well go unnoticed. Buyers blithely perform puppy tests without understanding what they're looking for, and more importantly, how to match the responses they get with the qualities they need/want in an adult dog.

Perhaps the biggest mistake buyers make is insisting on selecting the "best" puppy from a specific litter, disregarding the reality that that litter may not contain the puppy who has the qualities they want. The best of a given lot of puppies may not be the best puppy, no more than the best car on a used car lot is the car you actually want.

One of the agreements I have with all of my prospective puppy buyers is that I will not sell them a puppy unless I have one whose behavior and puppy test results match their criteria. Occasionally, when a buyer has very specific criteria, such as wanting a dog who can handle a highly competitive obedience career, this has meant waiting for another litter. While disappointing at times, my insistence on trying to match the correct puppy with the buyer has paid off. My puppies usually get the homes who appreciate their qualities, and buyers get the dog they wanted. When all you want is a pickup truck, it can be disconcerting - even dangerous - to end up with a high performance racing car, and vice versa.

While a proponent of puppy testing as a way of gathering information, I believe that such tests are merely confirmation of what a truly good breeder already knows about each individual puppy, assuming that the proper time has been taken to correctly socialize the puppies.

In the real world of dogs and breeding, this is a very big assumption. Often, puppies are not always raised by people who, though well intentioned, are as knowledgeable as they should be regarding canine developmental psychology and

Understanding Puppy Testing

techniques for maximizing each puppy's potential long before the testing date. Puppy testing allows an educated buyer at least a glimpse of what the puppy's potential may be - *IF the testing is done and interpreted by an experienced tester familiar not only with the buyer's particular needs, but also that particular breed and correct behavior/temperament for that breed.*

Like any test, a puppy aptitude test cannot be absolutely comprehensive but simply assesses particular qualities, skills or characteristics. And every test contains the interests and biases of the test designer. Regardless of which particular test you use, a little research into the test's background is necessary to understand the bias of the test's developer. A Schutzhund trainer's test may be very different from the guide dog trainer's - which in turn may be different from the obedience trainer's test, and so on.

It is important to be very clear what you are testing for. You may find that you need to alter your tests slightly, including some specific tests in order to evaluate certain characteristics. As a German Shepherd breeder, I have no need to assess the "birdiness" of my pups, but when I was breeding Brittanys with Kitty Murphy of Sequani Kennels, I made a point of evaluating the pups' reactions to a fluttering pheasant wing on fish line as well as to birds encountered while on walks with the litter or individual puppy.

Good, Bad & In Between

There is a wide range of possible responses from any given puppy, and there are breed differences which cannot be ignored. Within the desirable temperament of the adult dog of any breed, there is a range of acceptable variation. What might be an acceptable variation in a Shetland Sheepdog might be extremely atypical and undesirable in a Belgian Malinois. In my experience, these can be seen by a skilled tester.

For example, I once tested a litter of Pointers. Overall, these dogs were much "softer" in their responses than the majority of Shepherds I had tested. My interpretation of such responses had they been Shepherds would have been quite different, but as adults, Pointers and Shepherds display vastly different characteristics. There was one puppy who, when presented with the sight sensitivity test, stiffened, growled, crouched and leaped over 3 feet to grab it. Even when the rag stopped moving, this puppy continued to vigorously shake the rag and bite it.

Had this been a Shepherd from strong working or Schutzhund lines, I might have interpreted this response as an extremely high prey drive which would need careful training, and recommended placement in a home where this intensity could be correctly channeled and utilized. In a

Understanding Puppy Testing

Pointer, I considered it so atypical of the breed that it was "off the chart."

I warned the breeder that this dog should be re-tested, possibly not placed, and if they insisted on placing the puppy, it should not be in a home with young children. The breeder dismissed my evaluation with the comment, "He's just feeling frisky. He'll be fine." The puppy was placed in a family with young children, and was just over a year old when he was euthanized for repeated biting episodes. Unfortunately, this puppy treated any newcomer to the home much like he reacted to the rag - growl, leap and bite.

Could this dog have made a suitable companion if placed in the right home and given appropriate training? Perhaps. But the point is that the breeder disregarded information gathered in puppy testing - information that could have saved a lot of people and one dog a good deal of grief.

On the other hand, breeders often attempt to dismiss certain responses during testing as "well, that's in the breed standard." One working breed litter I tested was so unsocialized that they literally ran away from me when put down for the first test. I eventually gave up the notion of testing, and settled for observation of the litter at liberty. Sitting on the ground next to the breeder, whom the puppies adored, it was well over 20 minutes before any of the 10 puppies would approach me.

The breeder's response? "Well, this breed is supposed to be aloof. Perhaps you're not familiar with this breed." As a matter of fact, I had tested several litters of this breed, and had had at least 6 of this breed in my training classes in the last 3 years. Aloof? I could not consider tail tucked, wide-eyed panic fleeing from my presence as "aloof."

 Just One Look?

There is an unfortunate misconception that a single test is sufficient to evaluate a puppy. Dr. Ian Dunbar has repeatedly pointed out the absurdity of taking to heart the information gathered from a single test. Like any good scientist, he knows that repeatability of results is important when trying to determine whether a given behavior or characteristic was incidental to the moment or truly an inherent quality of that individual.

Understanding Puppy Testing

Dunbar recommends *five* separate tests, each performed by a different tester and in a new location for each test. Unfortunately, while I agree that multiple tests are best, it is difficult to carry out such a program given the time, energy and possibly money needed to arrange even a single puppy testing. At best, a seriously dedicated breeder looking to use puppy testing might be able to arrange for two tests, but in practice, I have not seen this very often.

 Nature vs. Nurture

Another problem with puppy testing as a predictor of adult behavior is that many behaviors in the adult dog are the result of age, experience, hormones and environmental influences. Obviously, no test of an 8 week old puppy can take these factors into account. While certain characteristics do have a high degree of inheritability, the degree to which these characteristics are expressed varies wildly as a result of environmental influences. As Pfaffenberger notes, "Once you have found the best puppies there is still the matter of environment."

I once tested a litter for a breeder of Golden Retrievers. Having read about puppy testing, the breeder was excited and asked to videotape the entire procedure for later review by himself and prospective puppy buyers. The litter had been raised in an active boarding kennel, and from 6 weeks onwards, had spent their days in a large exercise pen in the kennel's reception area so that clients dropping off or picking up their pets could socialize with the puppies.

With an excited grin, the breeder placed the first pup in front of me and exited the room. Through the curtains on the door, I could just see the video camera's lens moving and knew that he was focusing on the puppy. Unfortunately, the puppy took one look at me and fearfully disappeared behind the furniture. After several minutes, I was able to retrieve and attempt to go on to the next test, only to have him disappear again. And so it went, puppy after puppy, and dismayed, the breeder turned the camera off after the third pup. The best of the group was at least willing to approach me, though hesitantly.

Discussing the puppies' behavior over a cup of coffee, the breeder became somewhat annoyed with me when I pointed out that these puppies were considerably under socialized and that this would affect them as adult dogs. "But they've been out in the reception area every day for weeks! When people come in, they all run right over to say hello. How can they be undersocialized?"

Unfortunately for these puppies, this breeder, though well-intentioned and caring, did not understand the importance

Understanding Puppy Testing

of *individual* socialization and exposure to *multiple* environments both as a group and individually. He mistook the actions of the litter as a whole as indicative of the actions of each individual puppy.

Though he selected healthy breeding stock, provided loving care, good nutrition and medical attention, the environmental factors which could have enhanced his puppies' qualities were lacking. As adults, these dogs showed, in subtle and not so subtle ways, the effects of this environmental deprivation: they were easily stressed by changes in their environment or routine (though loving, friendly dogs), "stressed out" when at the vet's or groomer's (though that was chalked up to being just another "nutty retriever").

Fogle notes that "isolation for as little as a week during the socialization period results in impaired learning ability. The dog's mind is so affected that *changes are actually seen on his EEG.*" (Emphasis mine.)

And while Fogle is specifically addressing isolation, my experience leads me to believe that a lack of sufficient stimulation, whether emotional, physical or mental, will result in impaired learning ability and/or coping skills. Studies at Colorado State University point to the positive impact of handling and deliberate stressors, such as being turned upside down or placed briefly on a cool surface, on the puppy's ability to cope with stress as reflected in physiological changes in response to and recovery from such stress. (For more information on this study, I recommend "Developing High Achievers" by Dr. Carmen Battaglia, AKC Gazette 5/95.)

Putting aside his disappointment and upset, the breeder then asked how he could do better. After following my recommendations with his next litter, he called me to have that litter tested. Though genetically extremely close to the previous litter, there was a world of difference in these puppies. Confident, self assured and aware, these puppies were a delight to test.

Genetics or environment? The argument for nature vs. nuture is a lengthy and complicated one. My opinion and experience is that the greatest challenge of breeding lies in not simply selecting the best possible mixture of physical and emotional qualities, but in the brief 8 week period breeders are granted in which to influence and enhance those qualities so that the highest potential of each individual puppy may be realized.

Buyers should beware of falling into the trap of believing that once they get the puppy home, they can make up for any lack that may have occurred in the first 8 weeks. While you can make improvements, you cannot go backwards in time.

Understanding Puppy Testing

A puppy who has missed opportunities and experiences during the very critical first 8 weeks has missed them. Period. As a trainer once told me, "You can paint plywood to look like mahogany, but when it rains, it still acts like plywood."

 The Big Catch

While a valuable tool, puppy testing results are useful only when interpreted by an experienced tester. This does become a bit of a Catch-22 - how do you become experienced in puppy testing and interpretation without testing and interpreting? You don't. You have to do what everyone else has done - do it, again and again and again. And you have to learn, in depth, the basics and subtleties of your subject.

First, read and re-read everything in print on canine psychology, developmental periods, dog behavior, body language, puppy raising - and then read it again.
Understand and spend time with the breed - and dogs of all ages and bloodlines in that breed. Take notes. Follow up on dogs you've tested. Spend hours watching (not testing) puppies of all ages and breeds both individually and as a litter. Take a litter for a walk in the woods, or build them a

cardboard box maze, or create mountains and valleys with mounds of towels and some blankets - and then watch them carefully. Hone your observation skills. And practice.

If you are fortunate enough to find an experienced tester willing to work with you, spend time with them. Videotape each litter's test, and go over it with the tester, discussing it in detail. If possible, practice test puppies - that is, test with an experienced tester present to guide you through each test, explaining each response or their observations. (Obviously, such practice tests should not be used to actually evaluate the puppies involved since your timing, position or responses may not be right.) Correctly done, the testing procedure should not be upsetting to the puppies, and they will benefit from the handling experience while you learn.

Understanding Puppy Testing

PUPPY TESTING GUIDELINES

DO:

☑ Test no earlier than 49 days, no later than 10 weeks

☑ Use tester who is not familiar to the puppies

☑ Use a location that is unfamiliar to the puppies & as free as possible of distractions

☑ Test out of sight & sound of littermates, dam and other dogs, and people

☑ Retest 24-48 hours later if results are inconsistent or at odds with breeder's knowledge of pup

☑ Clip all toenails short 48 hours before test (be kind to your tester!)

☑ Be absolutely consistent with technique for each pup

DON'T:

✗ Have familiar people/breeder present

✗ Test with other dogs/littermates present

✗ Feed pups within 2 hours of testing

✗ Clip nails, give vaccinations, worm, bathe, do vet exam or other stressful activities less than 48 hours before test

YOU'LL NEED:

- Score sheets & pen
- Clock, watch or some way of judging time
- Metal bowl/pot & large spoon
- Crumpled paper balls (have several)
- Dishtowel or similar size rag on 6 ft. string
- Umbrella
- Optional:
    - Barrier for problem solving
    - Small plastic container & treat for persistence test

Understanding Puppy Testing

INDIVIDUAL TESTS:
Purpose, Techniques & Scoring

Described below are the tests, techniques and guidelines for scoring that I use in puppy testing. By and large, they are adapted from Wendy Volhard's test (which was created through a combination of the Campbell and Pfaffenberger tests). Be aware that all of the published tests offer neat, specific behaviors as possible responses - in real life, puppies often do things that are not exactly that neat. The skill in puppy testing lies in the scoring and interpretation of results.

For example, here are the responses of two real puppies to the Social Attraction test in which the tester simply calls the puppy to them. Puppy #1 looks up, sees the tester and gallops directly to the tester with tail up, and happily wiggles around. Puppy #2 looks up, sees the tester and saunters casually to the tester with tail up, and wags his tail happily. Both of these puppies would score a 3 - but there is a difference to be noted in the energy levels. How a high energy dog expresses his responses will be similar to but

Suzanne Clothier

perhaps quicker or more intense than the same basic behavioral response shown in a lower energy dog.

Throughout each puppy's test, the tester should pay attention to the overall attitude and energy level of the puppy. Perhaps this should be considered the gestalt perception of that puppy as a whole being, which is actually more than the simple sum of his individual responses. Never forget to look at the whole picture - this is a more valuable assessment than the narrowed focus on individual test responses.

For each test, I have defined my own particular procedure for testing. Refined over many years, I have settled on this style of testing as one that is neutral (neither encouraging, discouraging, threatening or overwhelming to the puppy), most likely to avoid inadvertent influence of the puppy's natural responses. Be careful of wanting to see a certain response and shaping the test towards that result - this is not uncommon when testers are looking for a puppy for themselves or when testing a litter owned by a good friend. It is difficult to have to accept that a puppy you were attracted to is not the right puppy for you, and worse yet to have to inform a friend that her puppies may not be all that she hoped. Also beware of entering the test situation with preconceived notions about a puppy. If you believe that Puppy A is a certain way, you may lose objectivity and fail to observe what is real for that puppy.

Understanding Puppy Testing

I have included "Watch for..." sections for each test. These are the subtle responses that for some reason are not included in most of the published puppy tests, yet are among the defining factors in deciding how a puppy's response should be scored. For example, on the Volhard's score sheet, a puppy who did not struggle during the elevation test might receive a score of 3. But a 5 also does not struggle. The difference? The 3 is "relaxed" and the 5 "froze." How do you tell the difference?

Not all puppies who offer no struggle are truly relaxed, though they may not be rigidly frozen (which is unmistakable.) The clue I suggest you watch for is heart rate. In a true 3 response, the heart rate may rise initially but settles quickly to calm and steady, but in a 5 response, the heartrate escalates noticeably, remaining elevated.

If you are unsure how to score a given response, simply write down a detailed note of what the puppy actually did, and go on with the tests. Often, when reviewed in the context of the overall test results and observation of the puppy as an individual, you'll get a better sense of what that response meant.

For my scoring purposes, I find it easiest to define a range of responses within a certain score, and will often mark a score with + or - marks. This reminds me that while technically a response fit within, say, the 3 range, it was close to the point where I might have scored it a 2, but missing some of the key ingredients of a true 2. I might mark that down as 3+ or even 3++. Sometimes puppies fall in between two scores - I'll mark those as 3/4 or 4/3, using the stronger tendencies as my top number. Thus a 3/4 is a stronger response than a 4/3.

While it would be convenient if puppies behaved according to clearly delineated recipes, they don't. Behavior is never a linear progression, but a gradation of responses. The trick in puppy testing is figuring out where on that gradual scale any particular response belongs. When in doubt, take notes and work from there.

Tests should be performed in the order given below. Notice that some tests are tied together - such as *Social Attraction* and *Following*, and *Restraint* and *Social Dominance*. The tester who calls a puppy to them and then stops to read or take notes before getting the puppy to follow may find that they've lost the puppy's attention. Upon releasing the puppy from the Restraint test, it is his *immediate* response that forms the Social Dominance test response, not what he does a minute later. These tests should be performed as one smooth test, without a break to take notes or decide what to do next.

Understanding Puppy Testing

SOCIAL ATTRACTION

Purpose: Determine pup's willingness/confidence in approaching stranger.

Technique: Pup is placed 4-6' from tester who is kneeling. Helper places pup facing tester and facing away from direction of entrance and immediately leaves, going out of sight of the puppy. Tester claps hands and calls puppy to them.

Watch For: Pups who prefer to explore room before responding to tester. This is not uncommon, though rarely seen on "score sheets" as a response, leaving many testers unsure as to the appropriate scoring and unsure how long to wait before scoring a "no response."

Many pups will first explore the environment with their nose before going to the tester. Tester should note in writing how far the pup is willing to work away from them, whether the pup uses the entire room or just a portion. Tester must also distinguish between avoidance or refusal to approach and exploration - look for and note contextual

Comes readily with tail/ears/body posture up & forward, jumps up, bites at hands	1
Comes readily, tail/ears up, paws, licks at hands	2
Comes readily, tail up, may wiggle a good deal upon reaching tester	3
Comes readily, tail down (ears may be back), quiet wiggling upon reaching tester	4
Comes hesitantly, tail/ears down, often makes an indirect approach to tester & lies down or becomes very quiet when tester is reached	5
Doesn't come at all, may actively avoid test	6
Explores first before coming to tester:	YES NO
If YES, for how long, and what portion of room is used (i.e., close to tester, explores entire room, etc.)	Notes:

Understanding Puppy Testing

clues - i.e., puppy appears confident and relaxed, using entire room or appears hesitant and only explores a small area near where he was left by helper. I do not consider this exploration undesirable, simply an individual characteristic to be taken into account when trying to match puppy and prospective owner.

The "explorer" pup will often spend as much as a minute or two sniffing around (which will seem like a much longer time to the tester), and then suddenly go to tester. Behavior at that time is what I score, but my notes on the delay are included and taken into consideration.

The pup who does not acknowledge tester in any way is scored accordingly. In my experience, a puppy who has not acknowledged the tester in some fashion within two minutes will probably be showing other contextual clues that he is uncomfortable approaching.

FOLLOWING

Purpose: Posture/behavior during following reveals degree of social confidence.

Technique: Once pup has come to tester (or tester has decided that the pup will not approach), the tester stands, getting and attempting to keep the pup's attention, and encourages the pup to follow by patting leg. I usually walk 6-10' depending on size of the room.

Watch for: Some puppies will very actively follow between your legs and feet and/or jumping up as you walk - be very careful not to trip or step on puppy. Tester should be alert to any signs of concern by the pup when the tester stands erect, as well as carefully observing the pup's posture while following.

Understanding Puppy Testing

Follows readily with tail/ears/body posture up & forward, jumps up, bites at feet, underfoot while tester is walking	1
Follows readily, tail/ears up, gets underfoot, may occasionally jump up or bite at feet	2
Follows readily, tail up, usually keeps up with tester or tries to	3
Follows readily, tail down (ears may be back), may follow slightly behind or to side of tester	4
Follows hesitantly, tail/ears down, often follows behind or at a distance from tester, may combine following & stopping	5
Does not follow at all	6

ELEVATION

Purpose: Response to situation where the pup has no control. This will be reflected in real life response to being crated, left alone, response to handling for grooming, vet care, etc.

Technique: With pup facing away from tester who is kneeling, tester interlaces hands under pup's ribcage just behind front legs, offering stable support and not compressing belly. Pup is lifted so all feet are off the floor by a few inches, and held there for 30 seconds. At end of 30 seconds, place pup gently on floor, but keep a hand on them for the next test.

Watch for: The position of the tester's hands allows for good monitoring of heart rate. Be aware that puppies who appear "calm" may actually be frozen - a stress response. The tester can feel this easily by the increased heart rate. A truly relaxed pup hangs quietly in your hands and the heartbeat remains steady and normal after an initial rise. A stressed pup's heart rate speeds up noticeably and remains elevated.

Understanding Puppy Testing

Muscle tone, breathing and toe position are also useful clues - shallow/quick breathing, tensed muscles and curled toes are signs of stress.

Tester should be in a comfortable position, supporting their arms by placing elbows on knees. Some large breeds are quite heavy, even at 7 weeks, and 30 seconds can get to be a long time to securely support the pup's weight, especially when the litter is a large one!

Very strong fierce struggles, growling, attempts to bite	1
Struggles fiercely, may vocalize in protest but does not growl or attempt to bite	2
Hangs relaxed without any struggle, head/eye movements calm, heartbeat steady	3
Settled but some struggle (either initially or towards end of 30 sec.), heartbeat elevated	4
Slight twisting struggle, heartbeat elevated, head/eye movement may be very still	5
No struggle, heartbeat elevated, limbs stiffened, "frozen"	6

Suzanne Clothier

RESTRAINT

Purpose: By placing the pup in a subordinate position, this test is highly indicative of the pup's social ranking, and thus predictive of pup's willingness to accept leadership and discipline.

Technique: Tester is kneeling. Using both hands, gently roll pup onto back (or side if pup struggles hard). For 30 seconds, hold pup in this position with both hands, not allowing the pup to brace against your legs. Tester's face should be over pup, in a *neutral* expression (neither stern nor smiling) with eye contact available IF THE PUP SEEKS IT. At no time does the tester attempt to force eye contact, nor does the tester respond in any way to the pup's struggles (either by talking, attempting to reassure or releasing the position.) This is a purely neutral restraint, not discipline. At end of 30 seconds, allow pup to roll over but *go directly to the next test.*

Watch for: As a practical tip, the tester may be very wise to choose a long sleeved shirt! Puppy nails can hurt, and occasional pups will attempt to bite your hands as well.

Understanding Puppy Testing

Tester should also be alert to changes in pup's breathing, heart rate, muscle tone & toes - a pup who lays calmly with steady heart rate and relaxed muscles is not the same as the pup who lays still with rapid heart rate, tensed muscles and shallow breathing.

Watch carefully for eye contact - this may be fleeting, as in the pup who glances up at the tester and then looks away, continuous, or avoided completely. As a rule, when restraining the puppy, I do not take my eyes off his face even for a second.

This presents a small practical problem - how do you know when 30 seconds is up? Either practice counting in a predictable manner (i.e., "one, one-thousand, two, one-thousand") that will be the same for each puppy, have someone make an unintrusive noise to signal time's up, or keep a watch/clock within your sight line. However you count your time, make it consistent for each puppy.

Screams, flails, tries to bite, struggle may be constant	1
Very vocal, struggles fiercely, may settle very briefly, may make strong eye contact throughout test	2
Combination of struggling and settling, may be vocal during struggles, usually makes some eye contact before or during settling	3
Some struggle, either initially or towards end of 30 second period. Heart rate steady or only slightly elevated.	4
No struggle. Heart rate steady or only slightly elevated.	5
No struggle, actively avoids eye contact by turning head away from tester, heart rate usually elevated	6

Understanding Puppy Testing

SOCIAL DOMINANCE
(Forgiveness)

Purpose: In conjunction with restraint, the pup's reaction here is reflective of acceptance of and acknowledgment of social ranking. I consider this "forgiveness" - how quickly does the dog accept and forgive being put in a subordinate position. A forgiving dog is more tolerant of handler errors.

Technique: Still kneeling, the tester allows pup to roll over from position used in the restraint test. Keeping one hand on the pup's chest to lightly hold him, tester uses other hand to stroke pup gently from head to tail until a clear response is seen. Tester also bends near to offer face to pup without forcing contact.

Watch for: Do not restrain pup who clearly demonstrates desire to leave by actively struggling against your hand - this is different from the pup who accepts the light restraint, offers response then chooses to leave. A pup who sits passively or without moving probably also showed signs of stress during restraint test. Be patient, and note how long it takes for this pup to return to normal.

Suzanne Clothier

Occasionally, severely stressed pups may take several minutes - this should be noted. I have had puppies who lay as though frozen after being released from the restraint test. One took close to three minutes to regain sufficient confidence to get to his feet.

Jumps up at tester's face, growls, may attempt to bite, may be vocal, whole body posture very up and forward	1
Jumps up at tester, may paw at face/hands, occasional nip in between licking face, watch tail/ears - often very up	2
Readily tries to kiss face, tail often wagging, ears often laid back	3
Wiggles around tester, licks hands, may try to cuddle under tester's chin	4
Rolls over, may lick hands, licking may not appear for several seconds, appears hesitant, ears and tail down	5
Freezes in place, or leaves, avoiding tester	6

Understanding Puppy Testing

RETRIEVE

Purpose: Demonstrates willingness to work with human. Of all the tests, guide dog organizations consider this one of the most critical and reliable predictors of working ability.

Technique: Using a crumpled ball of paper, tester tosses paper ball 2-3' in front of pup. The direction of the toss should be ahead of the pup, and in the direction he is facing, never towards the pup or perpendicular to his path. Once pup goes to ball, tester should remain quiet - "encouraging" the pup verbally can disrupt the pup's natural responses.

Watch for: Puppies do not have great eyesight at this age. Tester must be sure that the pup has seen the ball, and seen it while it was moving. If no response, toss the ball again, watching for signs that the pup has seen the object. I do not toss the ball more than three times. If I get a clear response, that's it. Repeated tosses are simply due to my uncertainty that the pup has seen the ball.

Chases ball, picks it up and runs away. Body posture up. May pounce on ball.	1
Chases ball, stands over it or moves slightly away from tester. Often makes eye contact with tester while "guarding" ball.	2
Chases ball and returns to tester without prompting. Note whether puppy returns *to* tester or simply goes back *near* tester.	3
Chases ball, may pick it up, but returns to tester without ball	4
Chases ball a little way, does not contact it, loses interest, may or may not return to tester. Some puppies may simply watch the ball with interest.	5
Does not chase ball, may actively avoid even watching ball rolling.	6

Understanding Puppy Testing

SOUND SENSITIVITY

Purpose: To evaluate the pup's response to a sudden, sharp noise. This test is very valuable when considering which home is appropriate for a particular pup. While sound sensitivity can be minimized, it is unfair to place a sound sensitive dog in a noisy environment, or expect this dog to be an unflappable performance dog.

Technique: Allow puppy to wander around room. With pup about 6' away and not looking at the tester, the tester sharply raps bowl/pan three times in quick succession with spoon. I do not rap the pan more than three times, and repeat the noise only if I do not get a clear response. Put pot behind your back for pups who insist on watching you.

Watch for: DO NOT scare the puppy by banging pan too close to them, or repeatedly banging. The tester should be absolutely alert to any response from the pup - often, this is not any more dramatic than the pup simply lifting his head and looking up briefly.

Testers should also be aware of the possibility that a puppy may be unilaterally or bilaterally deaf. A unilaterally deaf puppy may appear to respond normally. If you suspect deafness, continue on with the test, and do specific sound response testing at the conclusion of all other tests. Advise the breeder to have their veterinarian perform BAER testing if you suspect any degree of hearing problems.

Listens, locates, growls/barks at noise just before or while walking towards source. Body posture very up and forward.	1
Listens, locates, barks briefly, body posture up	2
Listens, locates and move towards source of sound without vocalizing, tail may come up	3
Listen, locates sound, little or no change in body posture other than ears up	4
Startles, backs away, body posture changes to defensive/submissive, ears/tail down, may try to hide	5
Ignores sound, no response/curiosity	6

Understanding Puppy Testing

SIGHT SENSITIVITY

Purpose: Test pup's reaction to visual stimuli. Like the sound sensitive dog, a pup who displays a high level of reactivity (fearful or aggressive) to visual stimuli needs to be carefully placed.

Technique: I use a dishcloth or similar sized rag tied on a 6 feet light weight rope or string. With the pup wandering around the room, gently toss the rag 3-6' feet in front of pup. Rag should NEVER be thrown towards pup, but perpendicular to or ahead of his direction of travel. Slowly drag the rag in a steady pull away from (never towards) the pup, noting his reaction from the time he sees it. Once the pup makes contact with the rag (either foot or mouth) stop pulling and observe the pup's response to the "dead" rag.

Watch for: Scaring the pup by throwing rag at him. Don't jerk or flutter rag to excite a response, and avoid playing tug of war - once the puppy makes contact, the rag should go dead.

The tester should note how long the puppy remains engaged with the rag after it has gone "dead" - some pups will continue to bite, shake, growl at or carry the rag while others lose interest immediately

Looks, body posture changes to very forward/up, attacks & bites, may vocalize with growling/barking, continues to shake/bite even rag stops moving	1
Looks, tail/ears/head up, follows with intensity, may bark & bite at rag, some interest/contact after rag stops moving	2
Follows rag with curiosity, tail up, tries to investigate, may mouth/bite rag, loses interest when it stops moving	3
May follow rag hesitantly, watch for tail/ears down, may bark or growl defensively while moving backwards from rag. May be bolder when rag has stopped moving.	4
Tail tucked, backs away, tries to hide.	5
Runs away, actively avoids rag.	6

Understanding Puppy Testing

STABILITY

Purpose: Test the pup's reaction to large, unstable & unfamiliar object.

Technique: With puppy about 6' away, SLOWLY open umbrella in a direction parallel with puppy's direction, and place it on its side on the floor. Allow puppy to investigate. Be sure to watch puppy's response from the moment you begin to open the umbrella until time puppy shows no further interest in or active avoidance of umbrella. BE SURE umbrella is locked into open position, and will not suddenly close or collapse on puppy.

Watch For: Avoid startling puppy by opening umbrella too fast, or pointing it at puppy while opening. Do not drop umbrella or allow it to whirl around on the floor - simply place it quietly on its side.

Responds with bark/growl, leaps at and bites umbrella. Body posture very up.	1
No startle, goes directly to umbrella, tail up, may mouth or bite umbrella, investigates by stepping on or into umbrella	2
No startle or very quick recovery, investigates boldly, tail up	3
Startles, recovers (more slowly than 3), tail rarely up, willing to investigate after recovery but usually from a distance and cautiously.	4
Startles, tail tucked, ears down, avoids umbrella, unwilling to investigate	5
Startles, run away, tries to hide, actively avoids umbrella	6

Understanding Puppy Testing

TOUCH SENSITIVITY

Purpose: Test puppy's response to unpleasant physical stimuli.

This can be highly breed specific - many sporting & terrier breeds have been specifically bred to have very high pain thresholds. However, it is also highly individual. Never assume that a certain breed will have a predictable response.

Like sound/sight sensitivity, knowing what the puppy's response to touch is can help owners choose appropriate training equipment and be aware of the fact that tactile signals such as collar/leash cues must be felt to be understood. Many dogs labeled "stubborn" or "stupid" are actually quite insensitive to physical stimuli and require alternative training approaches.

When placing a puppy in a household with children, a highly touch sensitive dog is a poor choice. Retrievers have traditionally been considered great "family" dogs in large part because of their low aggression levels and high degree of pain tolerance.

Technique: Gently holding the puppy securely supported in one arm, position your thumb and forefinger on the webbing between the front toes. Consider making contact with the webbing as 1, and very firm pressure as 10. Gradually increase the pressure as you count, noting at which count the puppy reacts. Once puppy has responded, take a moment to gently stroke the foot before putting the puppy down on the floor.

Watch For: The tester must distinguish between resentment of having feet handled with pain response. As a general rule, puppies who are simply resisting having their feet handled do so when the foot is held in any manner. Take a moment to calm the puppy and try again. Some puppies will not respond to pressure - no matter how hard you press, the puppy simply shows no response. Jokingly, I rate such dogs 15 on a scale of 1-10!

Understanding Puppy Testing

ENERGY LEVELS

While not a "test," an experienced tester observes the puppy's overall energy levels from the moment all testing begins. I rate puppies as:

- *Very high energy* - gallops just about everywhere
- *High energy* - trots constantly with occasional galloping
- *Medium energy* - trots with some walking
- *Low energy* - walks with some trotting

Combined with other factors, an assessment of energy levels can be extremely useful information. The elderly couple DOES NOT need the dog who gallops everywhere! Energy levels should also be assessed through repeated observations of the puppies individually in other settings and at other times, and within the litter setting. A puppy who lacks confidence in the testing situation may actually be a very high energy puppy in a more familiar environment. This puppy might be quiet and reserved in public, but hell on wheels at home with his family.

OTHER TESTS

Natural Inclination

If you have specific goals in mind, such as tracking, herding, agility, search & rescue, lure coursing or bird work, you may wish to design some tests that help you discover which puppies show natural inclinations towards that activity.

For example, a future agility dog should be willing to investigate and walk/play on unusual surfaces (such as plastic sheeting or an ex-pen), an unstable surface such as a plywood piece propped on a small block of wood so that it rocks slightly, etc.

A Portugese Water Dog breeder asked me to test his puppies' response to water, so we filled a child's wading pool and sat back to watch the litter's response. It was interesting to watch which puppies thought that water was a grand concept to be immediately explored, which puppies were curious but unsure about getting really wet, and which puppies preferred a "grandmother at the beach" approach in

Understanding Puppy Testing

which they dipped their front feet but resisted going further and drawing back when splashed by other pups.

Be careful not to give too much weight to your observations and making statements such as, "Oh, he just loves water - he'll make the best dog for water work!" or "He's fearless - he climbs on everything - there's your agility dog!" The pup who launches himself into the pool or fearlessly clambers over unusual surfaces might make a perfectly dreadful dog for your purposes if he's noise sensitive, or unwilling to work with humans, or highly independent, or poorly structured.

Natural inclination test results should be used as a final straw to tip you one way or the other on two equally well suited dogs. If both *equally* display the characteristics you are seeking and one shows a stronger natural inclination for the type of activities you have planned, then choose the pup who is showing you where his passion will lie.

While most dogs can learn to perform adequately in any activity given enough time and careful training, the wise puppy buyer and the wise breeder know that natural inclination can make the process not only easier, but ultimately a greater joy for the dog.

Persistence

My husband and I have done this persistence test while trying to decide between two fairly equal puppies for an obedience competitor in Seattle. Using an empty, clean margarine tub, we showed the puppy a treat, then placed it under the plastic tub. (These puppies already had some basic work in using their noses and came from lines known to be strong in terms of scenting ability - if your puppies do not, you might consider punching a few holes in the top and using a particularly fragrant treat like cheese or fresh cooked liver to insure their interest and motivation.)

We then sat back and observed how long each puppy was willing to work on this problem - the winner in this case was the puppy who happily worked for close to 9 minutes, actively pushing the container around and trying different approaches until at last he tipped the container over.

One mistake we made initially was having both of the candidates present. To our amusement, while the blue collared pup worked tirelessly for 9 minutes, his brother wearing the purple collar gave up actively working the container rather quickly but laid down to attentively watch his brother's efforts. When Blue finally succeeded in tipping the container over, Purple reached in calmly and ate the treat! After he did this twice, we smartened up and

Understanding Puppy Testing

removed Purple from the testing situation. When on his own, we discovered that Purple was perhaps best categorized as "management potential" - he liked to sit and watch others work then reap the benefits! His brother was willing to do the actual work.

As a note, the blue collar puppy went to Seattle to a man who had clearly asked for persistence as one of the qualities he was seeking. About 2 weeks after he got the puppy, he called to complain that the puppy was too persistent! Seems that the puppy thought very little of being left alone for a brief time in a spacious and interesting dog run, so he opened the gate and appeared at the back door. The owner changed the gate closure, but the puppy persisted until he had figured that one out as well - and appeared at the back door!

The final straw was when the puppy not only got out of the dog run, appeared at the back door and then decided his people were simply too slow in responding to his barks - and opened the back door and left himself in. That was the last time they tried to put Merlin in the dog run! As his owner admitted with a chuckle, "I asked for persistence, and I got it!"

In some situations, such as search & rescue and serious obedience competition, the puppy who met all other criteria and displayed excellent persistence would be our preferred choice over a less persistent puppy. Persistence alone is not a valid selection criteria.

 Problem Solving

For this test, use a 6-8' section (or more for puppies of very large or giant breeds) of any barrier that a puppy can see through but not get through. This barrier must be stable and not knocked over by a puppy actively jumping or pawing against it. Place the puppy at the halfway point of the barrier with the barrier between the tester and the puppy. The tester then backs away 5-6 feet and calls puppy to him.

Some puppies will try to go straight through the barrier and then sit there, frustrated and sometimes whining, barking or screaming. Other puppies begin to seek a solution to the problem by working along the fence until they reach the opening.

For this test, I would note the amount of time it took for the puppy to work out the problem (assuming they did.) I would consider the puppy "done" when he sits down or stops working to solve the problem and offers no other behaviors. Once the puppy is done, the tester should

Understanding Puppy Testing

approach the barrier and guide the puppy to a solution at either end.

I would repeat this test twice more, comparing the puppy's initial response to his subsequent responses. Some puppies will have the same response to each test, others will remember the solution they were shown.

For scoring purposes, I would rank responses in this order of *decreasing* desirability if independent problem solving is a desired quality:

1. *The puppy who independently solves the problem.* If more than one puppy fits the quality, and all other qualities are equal, I would rank slightly higher the puppy who solved the problem the quickest or with the least amount of effort.

I have seen puppies run up and down the barrier and ultimately solve the problem in the same amount of time as a puppy who sat calmly looking at the problem and then, after sufficient contemplation, go directly to a solution. This is a matter of personal preference - you may prefer a puppy who continually and actively works on a problem or a thoughtful thinker.

2. The one-trial learner who remembers the solution on the second and third tests

3. The puppy who is willing but unable to solve the problem without help or active encouragement

4. The puppy who has to work it out as if it were a new problem every time

5. The puppy who gives up on subsequent attempts, even when shown the solution in the first test

Understanding Puppy Testing

INTERPRETATION

When interpreting each individual puppy's score sheet, I do not consider the scores for touch sensitivity until after I've figured out what the overall trend is. Does the puppy score mostly 3's and 4's? Is he consistently 5's? Since many dogs would score a 1 on touch (that is, highly insensitive), this can throw off your first appraisal.

The following describe the pup who scored consistently in each category. Be aware that within each category, there remains a considerable range of highly individual personalities.

Give me four dogs that all had the same scores on their puppy tests, and I'll show you four very different dogs. Far too many influences, both intrinsic and extrinsic, are at work in the development of every dog as an unique individual for a cookie cutter approach. *Similarities in response* to certain situations are what puppy testing reveals.

Some discretion, knowledge of the breed, and an ability to blend the characteristics below are needed for an accurate appraisal. You must also add to this information the tester noted for heart rate/stress response, energy level and the results of any other tests you added.

Pups who do not show a tendency towards consistency may not be feeling well and should be re-tested 24 - 48 hours later before you make any decision. When in doubt, have a puppy retested several times by several different testers, and even consider altering the time of day of testing.

On occasion, I have seen puppies who repeatedly scored with results all over the board. One of these was in a litter I had about 10 years ago. Her behavior in the litter was consistent with what we saw on puppy tests - no predictable behavior pattern. I had this puppy euthanized. The veterinarian who did the autopsy felt that this puppy had neurological problems. This was not a surprise to me, and simply confirmed what I had intuitively known all along - something was not right.

While I do not believe in culling by euthanasia for cosmetic reasons, such as incorrect color/coat, I do believe that temperament is paramount. I would rather be sad about putting a puppy down than creating heartbreak and possible tragedy for a family who simply wanted a loving, stable dog.

Understanding Puppy Testing

Although it is difficult to do, sometimes the kindest thing for a puppy with erratic behavior or severe temperament problems is euthanasia. It is the breeder's responsibility to deal with the things that go bump in the dark night of breeding. Don't place unstable, unpredictable puppies with anyone.

Profiles of Puppy Personality

Mostly 1's

This is a highly independent dog, easily provoked to bite, with dominant & aggressive tendencies. This dog is usually unwilling to accept leadership, and even in experienced hands, is a difficult dog to train. There is no place for such a dog as a companion animal. I would be very cautious with any puppy who scored a 1 in any category except retrieving or touch.

Mostly 2's

This is a highly confident dog who can be provoked to bite. Often high energy, these pups are determined, intelligent and quick to take advantage of owner weaknesses. They are often described as "dogs with a mind of their own." This is an excellent working dog with resilience, though the handler must be unfailingly firm, consistent and fair. Especially in guarding breeds, pups who score mostly 2's need early and ongoing obedience training to avoid problem behavior in adolescence or early adulthood. A pup who scores 2's needs plenty of stimulation, exercise and mental workouts. This is an adaptable, confident dog who will do well at top levels of competition. Too active for older folks, and often too dominant for small children.

Mostly 3's

Confident, adaptable, energetic and willing to please, the pup who scores mostly 3's is usually a forgiving, happy worker. While they can be a bit pushy if allowed too much freedom, the mostly 3's dog is a dog who readily accepts *clear* leadership. These intelligent pups do well with an active family, and usually do well with children. They can be more active than some people might like. This pup would be a good choice for a handler interested in competition but not seeking the ultimate OTCH. Can be, with pressure, provoked to bite.

Understanding Puppy Testing

Mostly 4's

This pup is the dog who responds to any leadership, rarely pushing the limits within the household. Not as confident or adaptable as the pup who scores 3's, the pup who scores mostly 4's is an excellent choice for a family with younger children or an older couple. Energy levels are often lower with this profile. Socialization is critical to avoid this somewhat "soft" dog becoming fearful. These pups do very well in a fairly structured environment, and eager to please, are easily trained, readily forgiving handler error. This dog is not easily provoked to bite.

Mostly 5's

This is a very submissive dog, somewhat unstable dog. Socialization and confidence building are critical. Changes are stressful for this dog, and it takes a long time for this dog to adapt to new situations and surroundings. Under stress, this dog will bite defensively. This pup is a very bad choice for children, active households or anyone who wants an adaptable, outgoing dog.

In guarding & some herding breeds, I would consider this pup unacceptable. In some sporting & hound breeds, this temperament is not uncommon, and acceptable to owners who want little more from a dog than a household companion. No matter what breed, this pup is a poor choice for any competitive work, including the breed ring.

Mostly 6's

This is a dog who has little desire for human contact, and may actively avoid petting or affection. It is difficult to establish any relationship with this dog, and it may prefer other dogs to people. In my opinion, the pup who scores mostly 6's is unacceptable as a companion, breeding animal or working dog. If stressed, this pup will bite.

CONCLUSION

Puppy testing is far from an exact science. It requires patient observation, a willingness to accept what you see without excuse, preconceived notions or over-interpretation, and the grace to really listen to what a puppy can tell you about himself if you take the time to hear him.

Weigh carefully what you find. Know that certain characteristics are highly susceptible to environmental influences both before and after 8 weeks of age, some are strongly genetic, and some qualities are very difficult in certain combinations (for example, high energy, dominant and touch insensitive puppies often mature into "hard headed, stubborn, untrainables" unless they end up in the hands of a skilled trainer who understands how to work with these qualities.)

You may have noticed that all of the tests presented have to do with the puppy's mind and his emotional responses to certain situations. Please do not overlook the critical importance of the puppy's structure and suitability for the job you have in mind for him. No matter how wonderful a puppy's mind may be, no matter how much he displays to the utmost the attitude and intelligence you may be seeking, if that wonderful mind is housed in an inadequate body, you will be asking for more than any dog should be asked to give - something beyond his physical capabilities.

Know what correct, working structure is for your breed, and take the time to find the dog who is both structurally and mentally suited to fit your needs. Become knowledgeable about structural problems that can have serious impact on a dog's working ability. Recognize that a good breeder not only takes care of her puppies' minds, but also works to educate and enhance their bodies through challenges in the environment.

Take your time. "Act in haste, repent at leisure" is perhaps never more true than when acquiring a puppy. While I suppose you could simply get rid of a pup who didn't mature to your standards, far too much love and energy (not to mention hopes and dreams) goes into a puppy for most of us to easily discard a friend. This is a lifelong relationship and well worth a careful search.

For breeders, I would urge you to take seriously the results of your puppy testing. Of the many moral obligations we have when we bring puppies into this world, one of the greatest is our obligation to provide them not only with a good home, but a home in which their unique personalities,

Understanding Puppy Testing

quirks, needs and talents are appreciated, understood and allowed to blossom.

When trying to interpret the information you've accumulated from the puppy himself, keep in mind J. Allen Boone's wonderful quote from **Kinship With All Life**:

> *"There's facts about dogs, and opinions about dogs.*
> *If you want an opinion, ask a human.*
> *If you want the facts, ask a dog."*

Puppy testing has its limits. It is not an infallible predictor of the adult dog, but it is a useful glimpse at potential. Done with respect and attention, and used as a highly focused approach to observing puppies and their behavior, puppy testing offers another way to learn more about the endlessly fascinating dogs that share our lives. Enjoy - and don't forget to wear long sleeves!

PUPPY TESTING SCORE SHEET			
Date: Litter Owner:	Litter Date of Whelping: Tester:		
	Pup #	Pup #	Pup #
Social Attraction			
Following			
Elevation			
Restraint			
Social Dominance			
Retrieving			
Sound Sensitivity			
Sight Sensitivity			
Stability			
Touch Sensitivity			
Energy level, notes, recommendations:			

Understanding Puppy Testing

SOCIAL ATTRACTION	
Comes readily with tail/ears/body posture up & forward, jumps up, bites at hands	1
Comes readily, tail/ears up, paws, licks at hands	2
Comes readily, tail up, may wiggle a lot upon reaching tester	3
Comes readily, tail down (ears may be back), quiet wiggling upon reaching tester	4
Comes hesitantly, tail/ears down, often makes an indirect approach to tester & lies down or becomes very quiet when tester is reached	5
Doesn't come at all, may actively avoid test	6
Explores first before coming to tester:	
If YES, for how long, and what portion of room is used (i.e., close to tester, explores entire room, etc.)	
FOLLOWING	
Follows readily with tail/ears/body posture up & forward, jumps up, bites at feet, underfoot while tester is walking	1
Follows readily, tail/ears up, gets underfoot, may occasionally jump up or bite at feet	2
Follows readily, tail up, usually keeps up with tester or tries to	3
Follows readily, tail down (ears may be back), may follow slightly behind or to side of tester	4
Follows hesitantly, tail/ears down, often follows behind or at a distance from tester, may combine following & stopping	5
Does not follow at all	6

Suzanne Clothier

ELEVATION	
Very strong fierce struggles, growling, attempts to bite	1
Struggles fiercely, may vocalize in protest but does not growl or attempt to bite	2
Hangs relaxed without any struggle, head/eye movements calm, heartbeat steady	3
Settled but some struggle (either initially or towards end of 30 sec.), heartbeat elevated	4
Slight twisting struggle, heartbeat elevated, head/eye movement may be very still	5
No struggle, heartbeat elevated, limbs stiffened, "frozen"	6
RESTRAINT	
Screams, flails, tries to bite, struggle may be constant	1
Very vocal, struggles fiercely, may settle very briefly, may make strong eye contact throughout test	2
Combination of struggling and settling, may be vocal during struggles, usually makes some eye contact before or during settling	3
Some struggle, either initially or towards end of 30 second period. Heart rate steady or only slightly elevated.	4
No struggle. Heart rate steady or only slightly elevated.	5
No struggle, actively avoids eye contact by turning head away from tester, heart rate usually elevated	6

Understanding Puppy Testing

SOCIAL DOMINANCE	
Jumps up at tester's face, growls, may attempt to bite, may be vocal, whole body posture very up and forward	1
Jumps up at tester, may paw at face/hands, occasional nip in between licking face, watch tail/ears - often very up	2
Readily tries to kiss face, tail often wagging, ears often laid back	3
Wiggles around tester, licks hands, may try to cuddle under tester's chin	4
Rolls over, may lick hands, licking may not appear for several seconds, appears hesitant, ears and tail down	5
Freezes in place, or leaves, avoiding tester	6

RETRIEVING	
Chases ball, picks it up and runs away. Body posture up. May pounce on ball.	1
Chases ball, stands over it or moves slightly away from tester. Often makes eye contact with tester while "guarding" ball.	2
Chases ball and returns to tester without prompting. Note whether puppy returns *to* tester or simply goes back *near* tester.	3
Chases ball, may pick it up, but returns to tester without ball	4
Chases ball a little way, does not contact it, loses interest, may or may not return to tester. Some puppies may simply watch the ball with interest.	5
Does not chase ball, may actively avoid even watching ball rolling.	6

Suzanne Clothier

SOUND SENSITIVITY	
Listens, locates, growls/barks at noise just before or while walking towards source. Body posture very up and forward.	1
Listens, locates, barks briefly, body posture up	2
Listens, locates and move towards source of sound without vocalizing, tail may come up	3
Listen, locates sound, little or no change in body posture other than ears up	4
Startles, backs away, body posture changes to defensive/submissive, ears/tail down, may try to hide	5
Ignores sound, no response/curiosity	6

SIGHT SENSITIVITY	
Looks, body posture changes to very forward/up, attacks & bites, may vocalize with growling/barking, continues to shake/bite even rag stops moving	1
Looks, tail/ears/head up, follows with intensity, may bark & bite at rag, some interest/contact after rag stops moving	2
Follows rag with curiosity, tail up, tries to investigate, may mouth/bite rag, loses interest when it stops moving	3
May follow rag hesitantly, watch for tail/ears down, may bark or growl defensively while moving backwards from rag. May be bolder when rag has stopped moving.	4
Tail tucked, backs away, tries to hide.	5
Runs away, actively avoids rag.	6

Understanding Puppy Testing

STABILITY	
Responds with bark/growl, leaps at and bites umbrella. Body posture very up.	1
No startle, goes directly to umbrella, tail up, may mouth or bite umbrella, investigates by stepping on or into umbrella	2
No startle or very quick recovery, investigates boldly, tail up	3
Startles, recovers (more slowly than 3), tail rarely up, willing to investigate after recovery but usually from a distance and cautiously.	4
Startles, tail tucked, ears down, avoids umbrella, unwilling to investigate	5
Startles, run away, tries to hide, actively avoids umbrella	6

RECOMMENDED READING

The New Knowledge of Dog Behavior, Clarence Pfaffenberger, Howell Book House, 1963.

The Dog's Mind, Bruce Fogle, Howell Book House, 1992.

"A Novice Looks at Puppy Aptitude Testing," Melissa Bartlett, AKC Gazette, March 1979.

"Developing High Achievers" Dr. Carmen Battaglia, AKC Gazette, May 1995.